UNDERSTANDING GRATITUDE

Martina E. Faulkner MSW

INSPIREBYTES OMNI MEDIA

This publication is published and distributed worldwide in the English language in the following formats:

ISBN Paperback: 978-1-953445-78-0
ISBN E-Book: 978-1-953445-79-7

This book was printed in a manner that minimizes its impact on the planet and the environment. Learn more at: www.inspirebytes.com/why-we-publish-differently/

INSPIREBYTES OMNI MEDIA

Inspirebytes Omni Media LLC
PO Box 988
Wilmette, IL 60091

For more information, please visit www.inspirebytes.com
Graphics and photos: Canva Design Pro

"Gratitude is a virtue annexed to justice, because it is concerned with rendering to someone what is due to him on account of a benefit received."
— Thomas Aquinas —

"We should try by all means to be as grateful as possible.
For gratitude is a good thing for ourselves, in a sense in which justice,
that is commonly supposed to concern other persons, is not;
gratitude returns in large measure unto itself."
— Seneca —

"Thanks is given in three ways:
In heart, in words, and in deed."
— Thomas Aquinas —

Contents

> *"When I started counting my blessings, my whole life turned around."*
>
> — Willie Nelson —

Introduction

Gratitude is a topic that has been discussed throughout history. From philosophers to world leaders, everyone has an opinion and perspective to share. Going all the way back to Seneca (c. 4 BCE-65 CE) and Aquinas (1225-1274), we see gratitude tied to some measure of justice. Whereas in more recent years, Nelson Mandela defines gratitude as a "prescription," while Eckhart Tolle refers to it as a measurement of prosperity.

In short, gratitude is something that is often discussed, more often prescribed, and still too often misunderstood or misinterpreted. It is, in effect, one of the simplest things we can access (even children do it without being taught), and one of the hardest things to accurately define. This is because even though gratitude is universally expressed and universally understood, it's still incredibly personal.

So, what is gratitude, really? And, why do we need gratitude in our lives? Finally, how do we express gratitude? Is there a measure of gratitude that is universally accepted? All of these questions and more are the reason why we are still discussing gratitude today. Thankfully.

If you want a deeper understanding of gratitude and why creating a life that embodies gratitude is important, you will find answers in these pages. Truly understanding gratitude is about more than learning what it is; it's about knowing how to apply it in your own life to reap its many benefits.

What is Gratitude?

Though many have defined gratitude for millennia, the definitions usually focus on the effects of gratitude, or the act of gratitude, in relation to self or other. Being grateful, giving thanks, and showing appreciation are all ways we describe gratitude, and they are accurate in that they are synonyms. However, none of them actually get to the core of what gratitude really is. So, what is gratitude?

Gratitude is the feeling—and the tool—that takes you out of your head and into your heart.

There are two key aspects to that sentence: "feeling and tool" and "head to heart". By taking a deeper dive into why these points are important, we can truly begin to understand the power and potential of gratitude—as well as its true meaning in our lives, and, more importantly, how we can best employ it. So, let's break this down a bit further.

Gratitude as a Feeling

Gratitude is a state of being more than anything else—which means it's something you have to feel. Or rather, you get to feel, because it's a choice. Even though it is most often linked to an action, such as giving thanks or keeping a gratitude journal, ultimately, the most powerful form of gratitude occurs when it's felt. As a state of being, gratitude realizes its true potential when it is more than a phrase or an action, though those are often the easiest ways we can access gratitude, and they are subsequently, a good place to start.

"Gratitude can transform any situation. It alters your vibration, moving you from negative energy to positive. It's the quickest, easiest, most powerful way to effect change in your life."

— Oprah —

To better understand this, let's call gratitude the antidote to low frequency emotions, things like: fear, sadness, frustration, and anger. Like all good antidotes, they are most effective when applied quickly and deliberately. When our emotions develop frayed edges, gratitude becomes the balm that soothes. When we feel low, rough, or calloused, applying gratitude can help us shift out of that space and heal.

Gratitude becomes the tincture that helps to bring calm and peace to an otherwise overly active mind or body. It takes what is going on and almost alchemically transforms it into something else. In this way, gratitude is almost like magic. But, because it can be used tangibly and applied specifically, it's not magic. Instead, we can think of it as a form of medicine—one that brings focus back to the heart when we feel overwhelmed, scattered, or scared.

Gratitude as a Tool

As much as it is a state of being, gratitude is also a tool that can be used and practiced anywhere by anyone at any time for anything. This makes it universal... and incredibly powerful! As a universal tool, it is probably also the most expeditious tool we have. In other words, it can bring us back into a more peaceful and aligned state of being faster than almost anything else. Regardless of what you have going on, if you use gratitude as a tool to redirect your thoughts, it can take you out of virtually anything and help to restore balance. It does this almost instantly, too. As tools go, there are few (if any) that are faster.

Of course, there are many ways gratitude can be used as a tool, but the most commonly accepted method is probably keeping a gratitude journal. In a gratitude journal, a person typically writes down three things they are grateful for on a daily basis, often at the end of the day. By doing so, they are refocusing their thoughts to that which gives them peace, joy, or comfort and happiness before sleep. This focus just before bed will serve to shift the individual's presence over time. This means that, with time, their thoughts will slowly align to ones that are more heart-centered resulting in a more peaceful life.

As a tool, a gratitude journal is a relatively simple method that is available to anyone and everyone. As long as you have a method to capture your list, whether that's with pen and paper or by typing electronically, you can keep a gratitude journal.

"Something so simple, but it's important to take the time out from living and just appreciate what you've got right in front of you."

– L.A. Fiore –

The Journey from Head to Heart

The final aspect we need to focus on in the definition for gratitude is possibly the most important: The transference from head to heart. Why is this the most important piece to understand? Because it's ultimately what makes gratitude so powerful. It's the alchemy that gratitude gifts us, and it's potentially infinite in its application and results.

Now that we have differentiated between the feeling and tool aspects of gratitude, let's look at how they apply to the journey from the head to the heart. Whether felt or used as a tool, the result of being in gratitude is that your focus shifts from one that is thinking (and potentially over-processing) to one that is being. **When we are living from our heart center, we are more aligned with presence than when we live from our heads.**

Some liken this to the "gut feeling" we can get about something, even when our head disagrees. Though we say "gut" in that phrase, it's more similar to being in our heart. In a busy life and busy world, we can get too easily distracted by the noise and busy nature of things. As a result, we live in our heads more often than not, which has its benefits, but can also go awry. In our modern times, there needs to be a balance between head- and heart-centered living, and gratitude is the piece that can help to restore that balance when things have gone a bit wonky. It serves as a bridge between the two so that we can quickly and easily rebalance. We just have to remember that a) it's important to rebalance, b) it's possible to rebalance, and c) gratitude can help us rebalance, easily.

Understanding what gratitude means in reality is the first step to transforming your life. When you have a better grasp on how it can positively affect your life, you can begin to apply it in various situations and begin to reap its many benefits. In this way, it's also important to be authentic in your gratitude for it to work. So, let's look at what could undermine your practice of gratitude.

What Gratitude Isn't

"Silent gratitude isn't much use to anyone."

– Gertrude Stein –

Just as it's important to understand what gratitude is, it's also important to understand what it is not. Gratitude at its core is not about performance. When gratitude becomes performative, the lack of authenticity behind it can slowly erode trust and ultimately negatively impact relationships and circumstances.

We see this when acts of appreciation are generated automatically, such as with form letters thanking people for something. Yes, it's important to say thank you, and yes it is important to acknowledge gifts of any kind; however, when a thank you letter is generated repeatedly, without any effort to make a connection, the long-term result is usually one of disengagement.

We also see this when gratitude is imposed on someone, which can make it performative. Unless you're a child, being forced to say "thank you" or state something you're grateful for when you don't want to or don't feel it, undermines any connection that could have been possible otherwise. It's not actually gratitude if you're being forced or coerced to do it.

Just as gratitude isn't performative, it's also not an overture. This means that when gratitude is expected, an overture is usually made in an effort to meet expectations. This usually isn't authentic gratitude, but rather a form of appreciation. To understand the difference between gratitude and appreciation, try this exercise:

- Stand in front of the mirror and look at yourself, saying: "I appreciate you."
- Stand in front of a mirror and look at yourself, saying: "I am grateful for you."

Even if you can't put your finger on exactly why these two statements are not the same, you will be able to say you felt a difference. The undertone between the two is inherently different, as it is meant to be. While both are nice, gratitude feels more profound with deeper roots than appreciation.

Appreciation is often a form of expression that is done as part of an (unspoken) agreement; whereas gratitude is an expression of something altogether more personal.

"If the only prayer you ever say in your entire life is, 'thank you,' that will be enough."

— Meister Eckhart —

True transformative gratitude has to be real and come from your heart to be effective. To fully understand gratitude and its powerful role in our lives, we need to look at the effect it can have, both on ourselves and on others.

How Do We Express Gratitude?

> *"Showing gratitude is one of the simplest yet most powerful things humans can do for each other."*
>
> — Randy Pausch —

Ask anyone to define what an expression of gratitude is and you will come up with many similar answers, as well as a lot of different ones. This is because gratitude is both unique and universal. It's universal in our understanding of it when we see it in action, but it's inherently unique to each individual, as well as individual cultures, traditions, and practices.

So, how do we express gratitude? Is there a universal expression that we all understand, even one that comes from animals? And, perhaps more importantly, how do we receive gratitude? Can it ever backfire? Giving and receiving gratitude can vary from one person to another. Understanding that simple truth is key to understanding how we express—and accept—gratitude.

Expressing Gratitude

Gratitude has a few universal expressions that seem to transcend species, such as gift-giving.

For example, we have witnessed what we perceive as gratitude when a dolphin brings a sea cucumber to a human who saved his dolphin-friend from a net.

We have also seen other animals express gratitude, like when a cat gives you a "present" of a dead mouse at your feet or a crow brings little "gifts" to the human that fills the bird feeder. These gifts are a form of "thank you" from one being to another.

For humans, gifts can also be an expression of gratitude across cultures and traditions. For example, it may be a tradition to bring a "hostess gift" when attending an event at someone's house. Though gifts are universally accepted as a form of gratitude, not every gift serves this purpose or sends this message. In fact, there are traditions in which giving certain gifts is considered bad. For example, giving someone a sharp object, such as scissors or knives, is thought to bring bad luck and represents the severing of the relationship.

As such, expressions of gratitude need to encompass more than one method (such as gift-giving) and more typically involve an action of some kind. Across the world, gratitude can involve physical actions, such as handshakes, hugs, bows, and nods, to name a few. Or gratitude can be word-based, such as in letters or notes, speeches, or even multimedia messages like memes and posts on social media.

When looked at from this perspective, the potential ways to share our gratitude with others is almost limitless. The only constraints lie in the restrictions placed upon us by our resources, social norms, rules, or traditions.

Thus far, the focus has been on how we express gratitude to others, but what about simply feeling gratitude in our own lives? How do we express gratitude when it isn't directed at someone else, or even something else, like an event or situation? How do we express gratitude when we are alone or within the realm of our life? This is the type of gratitude that we will primarily focus on in this book, because this is the gratitude that can bring about the internal and external change that we seek.

This type of gratitude is less about acts of service or gift-giving (though you can certainly reward yourself with a gift for doing something or accomplishing something). Instead, the expressions of gratitude we make to ourselves involve thoughts and feelings. They involve a deliberate choice to shift our focus and perspective to get to a different place in our feelings.

"The miracle of gratitude is that it shifts your perception to such an extent that it changes the world you see."

– Dr. Robert Holden –

By expressing gratitude in this way, we don't have to attach it to a person or something external. Instead, we attach it to how we internalize things that are external. This means that we can identify something external for which we are grateful, but then bring it internally and give it meaning.

For example, if you express gratitude for air conditioning on a hot day, you may be identifying something external in your gratitude journal, but the feeling you are internalizing through this expression of gratitude goes well beyond the gratitude itself.

The meaning you attach to the feeling is what matters. Do you feel relief? Do you feel comfort? Do you feel joy? Whatever it is you are feeling amplifies the gratitude resulting in more high-frequency emotions, such as love, hope, and peace.

Have you ever seen someone cry tears of joy or gratitude? This is what it means to be fully grateful in your heart. Expressing gratitude is the gateway to other heart-centered feelings that can truly transform a life.

Expressing gratitude when you are alone can be a powerful exercise, one that rewards you with a happier, more balanced, and peaceful life. **To live a life of gratitude is to be in touch with your heart and make choices that reinforce that which brings you joy and makes your heart smile.** How you choose to express gratitude to others is one thing; how you choose to feel grateful within your own skin is entirely up to you—and it's the tool that changes everything.

"A grateful mind is a great mind, which eventually attracts to itself great things."

– Plato –

NOTE

What are "high-frequency emotions"? These are the emotions that we consider on the higher end of the spectrum from "positive" to "negative". Instead of labeling them "good" or "bad" (as no emotion has such inherent value), it's more accurate to say high- or low-frequency. In other words, they vibe higher on the spectrum, making them feel lighter or making us feel better.

Who Benefits from Gratitude?

"When we give cheerfully and accept gratefully, everyone is blessed."

— Maya Angelou —

We all benefit from engaging with gratitude. As much as it helps to improve our personal situation, it also helps to improve our lives and the lives of those around us.

This is primarily because of the rebalancing that happens between the head and the heart that we discussed previously. However, it's also because gratitude requires us to slow down a bit, which then allows us to engage more fully with life. The simple truth is: When we are less rushed, we are more present.

We can be our best selves when we incorporate a state of gratitude into our daily life. Being our best self means being the best version of who we are, or who we can be. We are human, and as such it's important to remember and understand that we are always evolving and growing. Also, as humans, we can make mistakes that cause problems and strife. We also experience problems and strife caused by others. **To expect a world without any form of struggle is to be a little bit blind to reality, for it is in the struggle that we grow the most.**

However, not all struggle needs to carry the same level of intensity.

In fact, when we are feeling low, we can sometimes attribute a higher level of intensity to the strife than what's warranted; this is where gratitude can help. A more grateful society creates less strife, overall, as well as less intense strife. A more grateful person is less likely to cause struggle for others, just as they are more likely to move through their own struggles with more ease. Intensity of the issue matters almost as much as the issue itself.

Gratitude, therefore, is one of the things that can help us experience our life with more grace, and even more joy.

When we can be our best version of ourselves by incorporating more gratitude, everyone benefits.

The entire planet and all species benefit from our engaging more with gratitude. How so, you may ask? How does a parrot in the Amazon or a koala in Australia benefit from humans being more grateful? The short answer is that everyone can benefit from the ripple-effect gratitude can have on life. It's a perspective that requires us to shift how we think about our own lives.

Consider this: If you are a pebble and you are thrown into water, you impact everything around you through a ripple effect. We know this to be true. The ripples may diminish in strength and size, but they still cause an effect. A ripple from a pebble will eventually reach a shore or bank. It may seem like nothing to a human, but an ant walking along a bit of dirt or sand might disagree when that tiny ripple raises the water level just enough to disturb the scent trail he's following, or to provide him with an easy drink on a hot day.

The simple truth is that there are no benign or neutral ripples. Every ripple has an effect and touches something, even if you don't see it yourself.

Now think about the pebble. If you are a clean pebble, you make ripples in the water without changing the constitution of the water itself. However, if you are a dirty pebble, when you hit the water some of the dirt is going to sluff off and be carried out into the ripples.

Though both scenarios cause ripples which have an effect, the dirty pebble is having a different effect because it has changed the water slightly. If you are the dirty pebble, the ripples you create often include some bit of the dirt you carry. We don't always think of that, but it's true. Again, perhaps this may be imperceptible to some, but it is nonetheless true that every ripple impacts its environment in some way.

We impact our environment in some way, every day.

"Human beings, by changing the inner attitudes of their minds, can change the outer aspects of their lives."

– William James –

This simple truth then applies to humans practicing gratitude. By incorporating gratitude into our every day presence, we get to minimize the amount of dirt we bring into the water. As a result, we can diminish the negative impact we have with the things we naturally create as humans. Gratitude creates cleaner versions of who we are—the person we bring into our environments.

Ultimately, this means that everyone and everything can benefit from gratitude. The water and everything our ripples touch can only benefit from our more balanced presence. As much as gratitude benefits us, personally, it also benefits everything around us. This, in turn, benefits us again, creating a cycle of positive reinforcement, and so on.

Though it may take time (and mass) for those ripples to have an effect on the parrot in the Amazon, the certainty is that they will, eventually. As long as we continue to focus on gratitude and move from our heads to our hearts, the choices we make will ultimately have a positive effect on the world around us. When we do so collectively, we can truly change the world for the better, benefitting everyone.

When Do We Need To Practice Gratitude?

"The number one joy indicator, the one thing that will predict whether someone feels joy in their life or not, is the practice of gratitude."

— John O'Leary —

Practicing gratitude can happen at any time. It can be anything from a daily, hourly, or weekly practice to something that you incorporate as part of your life and being as you move from moment to moment.

There is no one way to engage with gratitude; the benefit remains whether it is routine by design or more spontaneous. What is true is that the benefit increases the more you engage with gratitude. So, one possible answer to the question "when do we need to practice gratitude?" could simply be: Every time you think of it.

There are many helping professionals (therapists, coaches, teachers, gurus, etc.) who teach that gratitude needs to be a daily practice to realize its benefits. This is because creating a daily practice most often turns something into a habit, and habits are easier to maintain over time.

There is a history of using gratitude journals for this, which is great. In fact, there are a lot of people in the world today who practice gratitude on a daily basis through keeping a gratitude journal and there are a lot of options when it comes to journaling in this way.

Ultimately, whatever works for you to connect with gratitude is a wonderful place to start.

The frequency with which you engage in that practice is up to you. **In the end, the routine you can maintain is what you should be doing.**

If you can't maintain it, it isn't working for you and it's time to try something else.

Though keeping a gratitude journal can be really helpful, there is a difference between identifying gratitude and feeling gratitude. Keeping a journal and writing down what you are thankful for is not the same as deliberately pausing to feel what you are thankful for. In other words, there is a significant difference between stating what you are grateful for and actually being grateful.

So, if you keep a gratitude journal, the next step is to actually invite yourself to feel grateful after each item you enter.

For example, there is a difference between saying "I am grateful for a warm bed," and "thank you for this warm bed." The former keeps the gratitude in a more theoretical place (still partially in your head), whereas the latter places it fully in your heart. Try this exercise:

- The next time you have your favorite morning beverage (we will use tea in this example), hold it in your hands, and say aloud "I am grateful for tea," then take a sip.

- Pause.

- Now, hold the mug, look at the tea in your hands, and think about it for a moment. While still looking at the tea, say aloud, "Thank you," and take a sip.

The aspect of this exercise that most people struggle with is the lack of a specific person or object to thank when saying "thank you." But you don't need one to express this type of internalized gratitude.

As you do the exercise, the sense of gratitude will flood your heart regardless. **The key is to understand that being grateful feels different than identifying things to be grateful for.** When you do the exercise—when you experience the difference between stating gratitude and being grateful— you slow down. If you slow down enough, you will feel it in your heart. While keeping a gratitude journal is a good place to start, ultimately, the practice that will transform your life more completely and create stronger, more positive ripples in your life is one of feeling grateful.

The Good News!

The best news is that this is something you can do anytime, anywhere, for anything. There is no routine or task attached to it, because it's more than that. It becomes part of your life in a way that doesn't need you to create a habit or require a checklist. Eventually, being grateful is something you inherently are.

To get to that point, of course, you need to start somewhere. You need to engage in gratitude on a consistent basis in whatever way, with whatever timing, works for you. As long as it's authentic, and you invite yourself to feel grateful whenever you are identifying something to be grateful for, you will get there.

This means that the answer to "when do we need to practice gratitude?" will one day become:

All day, every day, because it's who I am.

"By writing what I was grateful for, I learned to look for things that made me smile."

— Dr. Ranjani Rao —

The best part about gratitude is that it can be practiced anywhere, anytime, for anything!

Gratitude is always available to you. Always, always, always. It is never not available. The beautiful thing is that you need nothing to allow yourself to access it. If you've grown accustomed to keeping a gratitude journal, it might feel as though you need the tools associated with journal-keeping in order to practice gratitude, but nothing could be further from the truth.

Ultimately, practicing gratitude is not just about stating what you're grateful for; it's about allowing yourself to feel, and feelings require nothing but your presence.

This means that you can engage with gratitude on any day, in any hour, or for any minute of your life. Sitting in a meeting at work? You can think for a second and remember that morning's coffee and feel grateful. Stuck in traffic? You can go into your mind and think of a song you love, and feel grateful.

Trying to organize your garage or attic?

You can look around you, see anything that gives you a smile, and feel grateful. The possibilities are endless.

Gratitude is not limited to the "big ticket" items in our life. Nor is it limited to the confines of a pen and paper or a keyboard. Gratitude is available to us every second of our lives. It's a choice we get to make. This is the best part about gratitude.

If you don't think it is available to you, stop what you are doing right now and look out a window or at something in your environment. Look at something that makes your heart smile and you will be in a state of gratitude.

You don't even need to say the words "I'm grateful for..." or "thank you."

You can feel gratitude just by looking at something or remembering something.

"There are so many things in the world that could be invisible to the material eye, and when you take a moment to stop, to pause, to be present and notice them—that's gratitude."

– Jay Shetty –

It is impossible to not be in a state of gratitude when you look at your life around you and find something that makes you smile. That is the beauty of gratitude: It is always available, and it can be done anywhere at any time for any reason about anything.

Gratitude is a Superpower

When you understand this, you can take it a step further when you realize that feeling gratitude and living from a state of gratitude is a form of superpower. It's amazing, because it's like having the ability to hot-wire your brain, your body, your soul, your heart, and your mind all at once.

There's a reason why a gratitude practice is often part of wellness programs; it's like having a secret key to unlock all the feel-good endorphins that we need (and a lot of people chase). How lucky you are to know that you don't have to "chase" anything — you just have to pause and invite yourself into a state of gratitude.

When you allow yourself to live from a state of gratitude, you create a healthier relationship with yourself, which can lead to healthier and happier relationships with others. It really is that powerful.

So, where can you practice gratitude? Anywhere and everywhere... and you should! Do it right now. Just look around you and find one thing, just one thing that makes your heart smile, and feel grateful for it. You'll be glad you did.

Why Is Gratitude Important?

"Behind every creative act is a statement of love. Every artistic creation is a statement of gratitude."

— Kilroy J. Oldster —

Gratitude changes your life completely. It is the one life hack that can instantly change everything, from how you're feeling to what you're thinking. Furthermore, over time, it shifts your perspective as well as your energy. The frequencies running through your body move in response to gratitude, for the better. This means that gratitude is important because we need gratitude both as a tool and as a way of being.

Life can be hard; gratitude can help make it easier.

Engaging with gratitude is also important because it does not require a lot of time or any special knowledge, effort, or understanding. Everybody knows what it means to feel thankful or express gratitude, even children and animals.

This makes it different from some of the other tools, perspectives, or studies that can change your life completely, like manifesting (which is great, but requires study to be effective).

Feeling gratitude is one thing you can do that will instantly change you. It changes your thinking, your feelings, your cells, even your face. When you are grateful, you smile more because you actually have happier chemicals running through your body. You show up differently, which can cause people around you to show up differently.

This is an important aspect of gratitude that isn't as frequently discussed.

When you practice gratitude, your world can change, and you need to allow it to happen. For example, people who are generally unkind may tend to fall away from your life because they struggle to be around somebody who is in a happier place. They haven't figured out how to be with someone who prioritizes their own well-being and it becomes uncomfortable for them, so they tend to go away. As much as it can hurt sometimes, you have to let them leave. They have their own journey to take.

Perhaps your example can serve to be an inspiration for them. Perhaps you changing your life for the better will give them permission to do the same. Or perhaps they're just not ready or in a place to want to change anything. All of this is okay.

Being in gratitude is always an internal job, because nobody can do it for you. Sometimes when a practice of gratitude is thrust upon you (such as during a dinner in which everyone is expected to cite something they are grateful for) it can feel false or inauthentic. It's okay to decline the practice in those instances, just as it's okay to participate. What matters is that you know that gratitude is personal and that your practice will always be unique to you.

What's most important is that you figure out how you can best engage with gratitude in a way that brings you to a place of actually embodying gratitude in your life, to living each day with gratitude as if it were part of the blood in your veins or the breath in your lungs. That's how important gratitude can be, and is.

> "So it is not happiness that makes us grateful.
>
> It's gratefulness that makes us happy."
>
> — David Steindl-Rast —

How Can You Find or Create Gratitude When Things Are Bad?

Though life can at times feel overwhelming, gratitude is always an option. Bad days happen, and bad things happen. We can never fully escape them. On those days, or in those circumstances, the key is to realize that you do not have to feel grateful for everything all the time. **When embodying gratitude is a challenge, you can make the decision to just focus on one thing at a time.** Instead of abandoning the practice completely, focus on the little things that bring you joy or make you feel grateful.

There is a simple trick to accomplish this when things are bad: You can create a prompt to remind you that gratitude exists as a tool—especially when access to the feeling of gratitude is difficult. There are many different things you can prompt yourself to do, including:

Listening to a meditation
Reading a book or journal
Attending a class, such as art or yoga
Calling a friend or loved one

The possibilities are seemingly endless. The goal is to engage in something that slows you down long enough to shift your focus and presence.

When you have done that, you can look around you and find something that makes you feel good. A reminder in your phone, for example, can go off at the same time every day prompting you to pause and look at your environment and find something that makes your heart smile.

"Gratitude is the memory of the heart."

— Jean-Baptiste Massieu —

When life is bad or when things are a struggle, if you can remind yourself to find something to engage with and feel grateful for you, it will help.

Gratitude is meant to be easy, so don't make it too hard. Keeping it simple will help you have more success. When we say to find something in your environment, it can be as simple as feeling grateful for air conditioning on a hot day, or ice in your water. It can also be as simple as somebody smiling at you at the checkout line in a store or seeing a dog walk down the street. It can even be as simple as enjoying a piece of chocolate or hearing birdsong in the morning or feeling the sun on your face.

To truly be in gratitude, you do not have to be grateful for winning the lottery or something else that is massive, heroic, or extraordinary. **In fact, it's gratitude that helps us see the everyday, ordinary things as extraordinary.** That is why when life is hard, engaging with gratitude can help make it a little easier.

Even on the smallest scale—for the most mundane things that you can think of, like warm socks on a cold day—gratitude is what changes things for the better. You just have to remember to look around you for a moment to access it.

How Do We Create A Life Of Gratitude?

A life of gratitude is created by choosing a place to start and then making a commitment to a practice. As we've already explored, this practice can be daily or not. It can even be multiple times a day. What matters is that it's something you can be consistent with, while also leaving room for flexibility and growth. In this way, you will create the most optimal situation for turning a practice into something you embody—something you become.

If you do it enough and make it a reflexive behavior, it will be something that changes your presence, until one day you realize that you just show up that way.

"Some people are always grumbling because roses have thorns. I am thankful that thorns have roses."

– Jean-Baptiste Alphonse Karr –

© 2025 Martina E. Faulkner

That's the important thing to note: A life of gratitude—an attitude of gratitude, as it's sometimes referred to—does not happen overnight. It requires commitment and a desire to change. Once you start down the path, as you begin to realize positive results from your efforts (such as feeling more inner peace or more joy), the process becomes self-reinforcing. It starts to feel like you can't imagine not living from a place of gratitude.

Once that has become your reality, you will know that you have truly created a life of gratitude, one in which you will always be able to find balance, calm, and joy. Though each path needs to be uniquely designed, here is a suggestion on how you can create a practice that leads to embodiment in three months:

Four Steps to Embodying Gratitude

STEP 1:

Start with a gratitude journal — Begin by writing down three things each night that you are grateful for. Be specific; for example, don't write "friends" but write down a specific friend and what they did or why you are grateful for them. Do this for 3-4 weeks.

STEP 2:

Add mornings to your practice — Start your day with gratitude. When you wake, carve out 15 minutes to revisit your list from the night before. When you do, sit with each item for a minute, allowing yourself to **feel** grateful again. Once you've done this, think of your day ahead and write down three things you are grateful for. Do this for 3-4 weeks.

Four Steps to Embodying Gratitude

(continued)

STEP 3:

Practice saying "thank you" — After 6-8 weeks of the journaling, add a new practice to your day, by specifically saying thank you. Sometime during your day when you are drinking something, pause, look at your beverage, and take a moment. After reflecting for a bit, say thank you. You do not have to say thank you to anyone or anything in particular; you are simply being in a state of gratitude for the beverage. You could be thanking the cow for the milk or yourself for hydrating with water. It doesn't matter. What matters is that you are deliberately putting yourself into a state of gratitude. Do this for another 3-4 weeks, while still journaling.

STEP 4:

Take stock and reflect — Look back on the 9-12 weeks of changes you have made, and reflect on what pieces made you feel more gratitude. Ask yourself what you would change. What would you do more of, or less of? Adjust accordingly.

Ultimately, gratitude starts as a choice. You have to choose to focus on gratitude before it can become a reflex. Furthermore, you have to choose it consistently over a period of time for it to become part of your being.

It's a choice only you can make (nobody can make it for you), but it's a choice that will be worth the effort.

> *"Gratitude is the power to connect with the cosmos and harness its energy."*
>
> — Sukant Ratnakar —

It's true that adopting gratitude as a way of being both benefits you and can positively impact your world, but what else can it do?

The short answer is: A lot.

Understanding gratitude and applying it in your life leads to more empathy, more connection, more compassion, and more empowerment, to name just a few of its benefits. These, in turn, lead to a stronger and better quality of life, which leads to healthier decisions, which leads to more investment in yourself and others, which leads to a better community, which can lead to better and healthier societies. And so on and so forth.

This, of course, doesn't happen overnight, but can happen in only a couple generations. The possibilities that gratitude can create are almost endless.

*Gratitude takes you from
your head to your heart.*

— Martina E. Faulkner —

Why Does Gratitude Create Endless Possibility?

As we said at the very beginning:

Gratitude takes you from your head to your heart.

Of course, the mind is a home for the entire range of emotions, from fear to love. It processes everything we are feeling and gives it meaning and significance, or not. The head is where we try to sort out our thoughts and our feelings simultaneously, often resulting in more confusion. When we say our "head was spinning" this is what we mean.

We are trying to make sense of something that we can't properly organize, mentally, emotionally, or intellectually. The mind will work overtime to try and accomplish this, as we cycle through more thoughts and more emotions as it churns. While the head processes all of our emotions, it is specifically the home for the low-frequency emotions, such as: fear, anger, frustration, hate, insecurity, annoyance, isolation, etc.

Conversely, these emotions rarely (if ever) reside in our hearts. Though the high frequency emotions can be present in the head, especially as you are trying to figure something out, they predominantly live in our hearts.

The main difference between the head and the heart, therefore, is that the heart is the home for high-frequency emotions, and these are the emotions that invite us to create a better world for ourselves and others.

When we are in our hearts, we make different decisions and ask different questions. We want to know how things will benefit others, not how we can avoid something. We ask proactive questions, rather than making reactive statements.

Living from the heart is what creates more connection and better solutions.

It's about recognizing that we are part of something, not apart from something.

It's the position that allows us to take perspective (which is a superpower), and build or create.

It's the realm of innovation, creativity, and of asking: **What's possible?**

"Acknowledging the good that you already have in your life is the foundation for all abundance."

— Eckhart Tolle —

Living From a Place of Gratitude

When we practice gratitude, and ultimately live from a place of gratitude, what we are doing is shifting to living from a heart-centered place—one where anything becomes possible because we are accessing the higher-frequency emotions on a regular basis while decreasing the low-frequency emotions.

So, what is possible with more gratitude?

The answer is simple: Everything.

Everything becomes possible with more gratitude, both personally and globally.

There's a reason videos of animals in the wild expressing gratitude go viral. We see it when a dolphin brings "presents" to someone that helped its mate get out of a fishing net or when a crow brings shiny gifts to a human that has fed it, for example.

We see it and we recognize it for what it is and it makes us feel good.

We feel happy because we know that someone made something better for someone else, and it was acknowledged with gratitude as a kindness received.

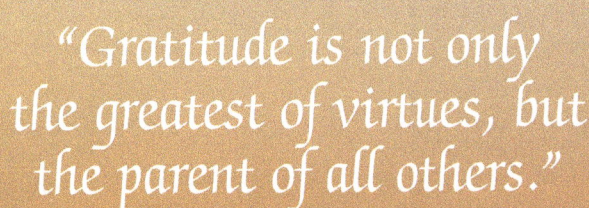

*"Gratitude is not only
the greatest of virtues, but
the parent of all others."*

— Cicero —

This creates a sense of goodness, which somewhat ties back to the philosophers that linked gratitude to justice. We know goodness and acts of kindness when we see them, and we like to reward them.

We reward them by expressing gratitude.

When we set up this cyclical system of goodness and gratitude, we are essentially building a kinder, more connected society.

In other words, gratitude helps to make better things possible... and maybe, even probable.

*"Piglet noticed that even though he
had a Very Small Heart, it could hold
a rather large amount of Gratitude."*

— A.A. Milne —

Conclusion

By now, hopefully you realize the power of gratitude and its incredible potential in your life. Understanding gratitude is, in some ways, about understanding how to create and live a better life, both individually and collectively.

We know that gratitude gives us instant access to higher-frequency emotions by moving us from our heads to our hearts. We also know that, to be most effective, gratitude can (and should) evolve from a habit or practice to an embodiment.

We need to adopt gratitude as a way of being in our lives in order to realize it fully. We do this by first creating a relationship with gratitude in our everyday lives. By identifying the things for which we are grateful, we can then learn how to express those feelings on a regular basis. We know that this will transform our lives for the better, sometimes resulting in changes in our relationships, which is okay. Ultimately, by embodying gratitude, we know that we can have a positive impact that has the potential to be far-reaching.

This is the good news of gratitude: The fact that something as simple as feeling grateful for the small everyday things in our lives can ultimately transform our world for the better. In that regard, gratitude, it seems, is more than a feeling or a tool, it's a way forward. It's a roadmap to a better world with more kindness and greater connection... one cup of tea or pair of socks, at a time!

 *"Those who find gratitude in the little things find humility in the big things."*

— Lidia Longorio —

"The quality of your life is based on the choices you make."

— Martina E. Faulkner —

About the Author

Martina E. Faulkner is a cross-genre author whose work focuses primarily on exploring what it means to be human, both the unique and the universal. She holds a trifecta in the mental health/healing world as a therapist, certified life coach, and Reiki Master Teacher. This distinctive background allows her to draw on her professional and personal experience in her writing, whether fiction, nonfiction, or poetry.

A self-proclaimed Anglophile, Martina drinks tea daily, loves walks in nature, and enjoys looking at beautiful images from the British Isles while dreaming up her next book. You can read her regular column ('Unique and Universal') on Substack, follow her on Instagram and Facebook @martinaefaulkner, or visit martinaefaulkner.com.

As a children's author Martina's debut children's book, <u>When the World Went Quiet</u>, was given as a gift to Sir David Attenborough, who referred to it as "charming."

<u>Other Books</u>

Understanding Grief
Understanding Karma
50 and F*ck It!
What if..?
Love and Pain
Infinite In My Heart
Me: 365
The Author's Journey
Crafting the Perfect College Essay

<u>Children's Books</u>

When the World Went Quiet
Princess Wigglebottom and the Forgotten Christmas

About Gratitude Journals

"I am happy because I'm grateful. I choose to be grateful. That gratitude allows me to be happy."

— Will Arnett —

Why Keep a Journal?

Keeping a gratitude journal is about giving yourself a gift. It's a gift of time and presence that results in more happiness and more inner peace. Making a choice to do something with attention can only benefit you in the long run.

More importantly, it doesn't have to be hard or complicated. In fact, it's often easier to keep up with a daily practice when you make it simple and/or fun! Whether it's saying thank you, or simply noticing things around you that make you smile, you can start or end your day with gratitude.

Make It Easy

When something is easier to do, you are more likely to do it, especially if you can feel the results easily, too. To practice gratitude, you don't need to buy an expensive journal or change your schedule; you simply need to set a reminder until it becomes a habit. You can put an "alarm" in your phone to accomplish this, or add the practice to your morning or evening routine, when you're brushing your teeth, for example.

If you don't know where to start, the following page is an example of a simple gratitude journal page that you can use. You can copy it, print it out, or even tear it out of this book. Or, you can simply create your own, using it as a guide.

However you choose to start your gratitude practice, you can't go wrong. The important thing is to start.

PS: THANK YOU for being here.

Scan the QR Code to download a PDF of the journal page

My Daily Dose of Gratitude for: _____

Embodying gratitude is made easeier by simply saying: "Thank you."

THANK YOU FOR...

1. _____
   _____

2. _____
   _____

3. _____
   _____

*"The more you practice the art of thankfulness,
the more you have to be thankful for."*

– Norman Vincent Peale –

OR, IF TODAY WASN'T THE BEST OF DAYS...

On less-good days, it can be hard to find things that inspire gratitude. So, let's make it easy. Take a look around you right now and note three things that make you smile.

1. _____

2. _____

3. _____